Lonely Elijah and the Little People

Words by Norman C. Habel
Pictures by Jim Roberts

Concordia Publishing House

A PURPLE PUZZLE TREE BOOK
COPYRIGHT © 1972 CONCORDIA PUBLISHING HOUSE, ST. LOUIS, MISSOURI
CONCORDIA PUBLISHING HOUSE LTD., LONDON, E. C. 1
MANUFACTURED IN THE UNITED STATES OF AMERICA
ALL RIGHTS RESERVED
ISBN 0-570-06522-4

Riddle me, riddle me, ree!
There's something that I can see.
If I look in a glass,
I can see a small face
that looks like a someone called *me*.

Riddle me, riddle me, ree!
Who is this someone called *me*?
It's hard to explain
why God in His brain
made me the small me that is me.

Did you ever wonder
why God made you to be you
and not someone else?
Do you think it's a miracle
that God has a plan for you
no matter how small you seem?

Well, that's the lesson
Elijah had to learn.
For Elijah was a lonely prophet
who needed little people
to help him understand just who he was
and what his God was doing.

When a great drought came,
Elijah was very hungry
and very, very thirsty.
One day he came to a town

with the strange name of Zarephath.
There he met a widow
who was just a little person
like any one of us.
She was out collecting sticks
to make a little fire in her house.

Elijah said,
"Could I have some water, please?
  I'm very hot and dry."
The widow replied,
"Sir, come with me
  and you can get a drink."

Elijah said,
"May I have some bread?
  I'm very hungry, too."
The widow replied,
"Sir, we only have a little flour
  and very little oil."

Elijah said,
"Please, bake a cake
  and God will bless us all."
The widow replied,
"That's all there is to eat.
  When that is gone,
  my son and I will die."

Elijah said, "Oh, no!
For God will make your flour grow
and your pot of oil as well,
because you've been so kind."

As the widow made the cake,
she said, "It's like a miracle.
The flour keeps on growing
and my pot of oil as well."

If you think you've never seen
a miracle like that,
then look inside your kitchen.
There's always bread
for God to do His miracles
through your mother and her love.

One day the widow's son fell ill
and died quite suddenly.
No one knew just why.

Then the widow said, "Elijah,
why did you make this happen?
Were you sent to punish me
for something that I did?"

Elijah replied, "No!
God doesn't punish people like that.
There must be another reason."
The widow cried, "Sir,
I want my son to live."
Elijah replied,
"Give your son to me.
I'll take him to his room."
The widow cried,
"Sir, my son is dead.
It's much too late for bed."

But Elijah took the boy
and laid him on the bed.
He prayed to God and asked,
"Why did You let this happen
to this lonely little widow?"

Then Elijah lay upon the boy
and put his mouth upon the mouth
of the dead little boy,
just the way that people do
when a little boy has drowned.
He breathed into the boy's mouth
and blew and blew and blew
until the boy was breathing
just like you and you and you!

If you want to hear that miracle,
just listen to yourself.
Then take a real deep breath
and feel the miracle of God
making you alive with air
and filling you with love.
Then you'll learn
what old Elijah learned
from a very little boy.

But Elijah was a lonely prophet,
for the people worshiped Baal,
and Jezebel, the queen,
prayed for him to die.

So Elijah sat in a cave
deep in a mighty mountain
and wished that he could die.

Suddenly the wind began to whistle
and scream and leap around
like a wild, ferocious animal
tearing up the ground.
But God didn't say a word.
in that wild, wild wind.

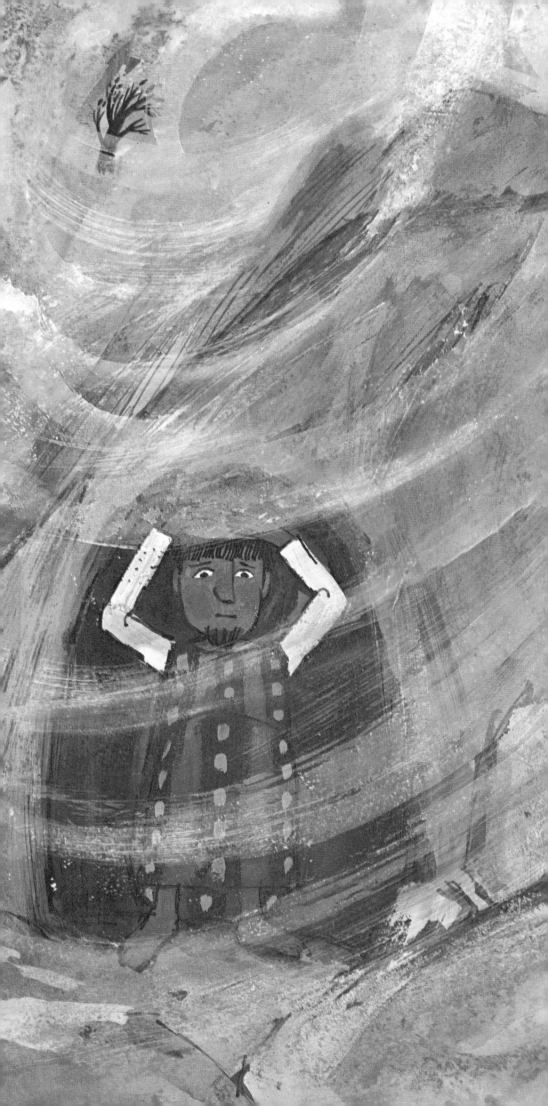

Suddenly the mountain began to grumble,
to mutter, to churn and shake,
like a wild, ferocious dinosaur
making a big earthquake.
But God didn't say a word
in that big earthquake.

Suddenly the fire began to crackle
and dance around the cave,
like a wild, ferocious octopus
with tentacles of flame.
But God didn't say a word
in that fierce, roaring fire.

Then the cave was silent.
SHHHHHH. Listen!
Even the bats are quiet.

Then softly, so softly,
Elijah heard a quiet, little voice
speaking to his heart.
Who do you think it was?

"Elijah," whispered the voice,
"what are you doing here?"

"I'm the only one who still loves God,
 the only one in the world," he said.
"And now they want to kill me."

Then the voice of God replied,
"Don't feel sorry for yourself
 just because you're you.
There are 7,000 little people
who haven't worshiped Baal
or kissed his big bull face.
Go home and preach My Word
about My love for little men.
Although My purple puzzle
may seem to be a fizzle,
I will always find someone like you
to end the plan I have begun."

So riddle me, riddle me, ree!
Don't say, "I am sorry for me."
The love that you do
because you are you
is part of God's big puzzle tree.

OTHER TITLES

the PURPLE PUZZLE TREE